Chapter 1: Introduction 6
   History 6
   Purpose 6
   Preventative Maintenance 7
   Restorative Maintenance 8

Chapter 2: Basic Troubleshooting and Fault Finding 9
   Checking Apparent Power 9
   Voltage Values 9
   Checking Connections 10

Chapter 3: Safety Guidelines 11
   Precautionary Measures 11
   Discharge Equipment 11
   Wear Eye Protection 11

Chapter 4: Radio Design Basics 13
   Transistors 13
   Vacuum Tubes 13
   Tuning Circuits 14
   Frequency Control Elements 14

Chapter 5: Testing Procedures 15
   Testing Routine 15
   Results Analysis 15
   Reports and Documentation 16

Chapter 6: Component Replacement 17
   Removing and Replacing Electrical Components 17
   Replacing Paper and Wax Resistors 17
   Replacing and Cleaning Pots, Volume Knobs and Switches 18
   Polishing 19

Chapter 7: Tools of the Trade 21
   Soldering Irons 21
   Desoldering Tools 21
   Testing Equipment 22
   Diagnostic Tools 22

Chapter 8: Interpreting Documentation 24

Locating and Analyzing Service Manuals 24
Operating Instructions 24
Chapter 9: Best Practices for Handling and Storing Parts 26
Managing Stock 26
Labeling Parts 26
Cleaning Components 27
Chapter 10: Disassembling and Assessing 28
Dismantling the Radio 28
Assessing to Determine Scope of Work 29
Chapter 11: Restoring Wood Cabinets and Knobs 30
Raw Materials 30
Finishing Materials 30
Process Overview 31
Chapter 12: Wiring the Attic Antique 33
Removing and Replacing Bad Wiring 33
Lugging Connections 33
Agraffes 34
Chapter 13: Soldering 35
Proper Temperature Settings 35
Wire Soldering 35
Gently Removing Old Connections 36
Chapter 14: Installing Tubes and Resistors 37
Installing Cooling Fan 37
Replacing Old Second-hand Tubes 37
Resistance Values 38
Chapter 15: Re-capping 39
Replacing Capacitors 39
Observing Polarity 39
Rerouting Power 40
Chapter 16: Re-Aligning the Radio 41
Calibration and Re-Alignment 41
Adjusting for Spectrum Balance 42
Chapter 17: Final Touches 43
Cleaning 43
Final Tuning 43
Inspecting Connections 43

Rejuvenating Motors 44
Chapter 18: Final Performance Tests **45**
Performance Measurements 45
Enhancements 45
Quality Control Protocols 46
Chapter 19: Cleaning and Lubricating **47**
Cleaning Gears and Galvanic Cells 47
Oiling Motors 47
Lubricating Controls and Switches 48
Chapter 20: A Deeper Look at Tuning Circuits **49**
Understanding Frequency Control Elements 49
Tuning Capacitors 49
Chapter 21: Testing with a Signal Source **51**
Signal Source Requirements 51
Utilizing a Signal Generator 51
Employing Oscilloscope 52
Chapter 22: Testing Radio Output **53**
Alignment Requirements 53
Resistance Checks 53
Power Testing 54
Chapter 23: Repairing Mechanical Components **55**
Fixing Tuners and Bands 55
Fixing Belts and Spools 55
Fixing Springs and Clips 56
Chapter 24: Adding Accessories **57**
Adding Markers and Meters 57
Assuring Voltage Steps 57
Connecting Phonographs 58
Chapter 25: Avoiding Disaster **59**
Applying Adequate Mounting 59
Avoiding Risky Alternatives 59
Controlling Heat 60
Chapter 26: Dial Scales **61**
Antiquated Dial Scales 61
Restoration Tips and Solutions 61
Chapter 27: Replacing Resistors **63**

Selecting Appropriate Resistors	63
Measuring Resistors	63

Chapter 28: Design Considerations ... 65
Tube Topologies	65
Shunts	65
Power Supply	66

Chapter 29: Advanced Troubleshooting ... 67
Paralleling Components	67
Troubleshooting Techniques	67
Hotspots	68
Hidden Faults	68

Chapter 30: Troubleshooting Tube Radios ... 70
Valving Sequence	70
Socket Tests	70
Optimum Conditions	71

Chapter 31: Troubleshooting Valve Amplifiers ... 72
Reactances	72
Adjusting Voltages	72
Resonance And Feedback	73

Chapter 32: Distortion Identification ... 74
Types of Distortion	74
Resolving Issues with Output Transformers	74

Chapter 33: Valving Modification ... 76
Re-Biasing Circuits	76
Troubleshooting Poor Valving	76
Employing Spray Cleaners	77

Chapter 34: Solving Common Problems ... 78
SWR Issues	78
Bad Connections	78
Blown Fuses	79

Chapter 35: Repairing Capacitors ... 80
Checking for Faulty or Leaky Capacitors	80
Replacing Capacitors	80

Chapter 1: Introduction

Antique radios have been around for generations, providing the entertainment and knowledge of generations past. Those who enjoy the mechanics of antique radios often find themselves in the exquisite process of antique radio restoration. Restoring an antique radio to its former glory may seem like an overwhelming task, but with the right knowledge and supplies, radio experts around the world are able to bring these historical objects back to life. Antique radio restoration involves a number of techniques, processes, and procedures that, when completed correctly, can provide a well-tuned, functional radio. To ensure the longevity of an antique radio, a number of precautionary measures must be taken throughout the restoration process. As such, it is important to understand the primary purposes of antique radio restoration before starting a project.

History

As technology has advanced, so too has our understanding of electronics and the use of electricity. From the early days of Marconi, Ferraris, and Tesla, the development of radio technology has enabled us to communicate across vast distances. The first successful radio receiver was developed in the early 1900's and was the primary form of communication through the 1920's. This gave the general public the ability to hear both local and distant broadcasts on their own radios. By the 1940's and 1950's, the size and power of radio transmitters and receivers was drastically reduced. This miniaturization, combined with the introduction of transistors, created a much more compact and powerful form of broadcast radio. Many of these radios are considered antiques now, as they have been outdated by more technological advances.

Purpose

The purpose of antique radio restoration is twofold. The first purpose is to restore the radio to its original glory, with all of its original parts and performance. This involves using the correct parts and procedures to return it to its original functionality. The second, and more important, purpose of antique radio restoration is to prevent further damage to the radio. Restoration techniques and practices help to ensure that an antique radio will remain functioning for many years to come. This can be done through preventative maintenance, which is primarily focused on ensuring that the components are still functioning correctly. This includes regularly cleaning and inspecting all of the major components of the radio, as they are prone to wear and tear over time. It also includes the preventive replacement of components that have begun to malfunction, such as tubes and tuned components. Restorative maintenance is another essential part of antique radio restoration. This is focused on the long-term maintenance of the plane, and covers a variety of techniques and procedures. These techniques include troubleshooting and fault finding, replacing parts, re-capping, re-aligning, and replacing dial scales.

Preventative Maintenance

Preventative maintenance is key to keeping antique radios functioning properly. Proper cleaning and inspection is essential to keeping a radio in top working condition. Cleaning should be done with a damp cloth to avoid any short circuits and water damage. During the cleaning process, familiarize yourself with the different parts and their functions. This will help you to prevent any issues that arise in the radio due to wear and tear. When cleaning and inspecting a radio, focus on the dial scales, knobs, and controls. Dial scales are especially important, as they are one of the most likely components to wear out over time. Cleaning and lubricating components on antique radios also helps reduce wear. If a component is worn out or broken, it should be carefully replaced with a new one. If the component is a tube, be sure to use the same type as the original for compatibility.

Restorative Maintenance

Restorative maintenance is concerned with bringing an antique radio back to its working condition. This involves a variety of techniques and procedures, such as troubleshooting and fault finding, replacing parts, re-capping, re-aligning, adding accessories, and replacing dial scales. Troubleshooting and fault finding involve finding out what is wrong with the radio and determining the cause of the issue.

It is important to have a good understanding of the radio's circuitry and components in order to accurately identify and solve the problem. Once the underlying cause of the problem is identified, the appropriate steps should be taken to restore the radio. Depending on the problem, this may involve replacing parts, such as tubes, resistors, and capacitors. It may also involve re-capping and re-aligning the radio. The key to successfully restoring a radio is to have a good understanding of the radio's components, circuitry, and schematics. Finally, it is important to customize the restoration to make it your own. This may include adding accessories, such as headphone jacks, or modifying the circuitry to improve the audio or bass. Adding or replacing dial scales or knobs can also be a nice touch, as well as repainting or refurnishing the wood cabinet. Whether you're attempting to restore a vintage unit or tune up an antique radio, the proper techniques, processes, and procedures of antique radio restoration should be followed. With attention to detail and a thorough understanding of the mechanics of the radio, you can give historical objects a second chance at life.

Chapter 2: Basic Troubleshooting and Fault Finding

One of the most important steps in antique radio restoration is troubleshooting and fault finding, as these techniques can help diagnose problems with a radio and identify any critical components that need to be repaired or replaced. Although older radios may not be built with the most advanced technology, the principles of troubleshooting and fault finding remain the same. In this chapter, we will look at the basic tools and techniques for locating and repairing faults in antique radio systems.

Checking Apparent Power

The first step in troubleshooting an antique radio system is to check and verify the apparent power of the device. Apparent power is the combination of the real power, or the actual electrical power that is being used, and the reactive power, which is the power that is wasted due to any frequency losses. Measuring the apparent power of a radio system will help determine if there is an issue with the device's power supply, and this can be done with a basic multimeter. Using the multimeter, set the device to voltage measurements, and then connect the probes to the power terminals on the radio. Depending on the model of the radio, you may need to refer to the user manual to determine which points to connect. After this, the multimeter should give you readings for the voltage and current in the system. With this data, it's then possible to calculate the apparent power of the device to determine if the power supply is functioning correctly.

Voltage Values

Apart from determining the apparent power, one should also carefully check the voltage values of the individual components in the system. This is an important part of fault finding as it can help identify any parts that may be faulty or not working correctly. To do this, a multimeter can be used to measure the voltage levels at various points in the system. For example, if the radio has a volume control dial, you should use a multimeter to measure the voltage across the terminals on the dial. If the voltage at the terminals is different to the expected value, it could mean that the control is not functioning correctly and needs to be replaced. The same technique can be applied to other parts of the radio such as the power switch, on/off switch, and any other devices that may be present.

Checking Connections

Another useful tool for troubleshooting and fault finding is an ohmmeter. This device measures resistance between two points, which can help diagnose any bad connections or faulty components that may be present in the system. To use an ohmmeter, simply connect the probes to the terminals of any parts that may be displaying faults or behaving unexpectedly. The ohmmeter should then display a reading of the resistance between the points. If the resistance is zero or close to zero, it could mean that the component is faulty and will need to be replaced. On the other hand, if the resistance is too high, it could indicate a bad connection, which can be remedied by cleaning the contact terminals and reconfiguring the connections. Troubleshooting and fault finding can be a complex process, but by using the tools and techniques outlined in this chapter, you should be able to diagnose any issues with your antique radio system and repair them to make the device work as good as new.

Chapter 3: Safety Guidelines

When it comes to antique radio restoration, it is essential to observe basic safety rules and guidelines. This is to ensure your own safety and the safety and care of the valuable vintage equipment. Radio enthusiasts should be especially diligent in following safety protocols, as antique radios can contain a number of potentially hazardous components, such as capacitors and circuit boards that contain lead.

Precautionary Measures

When attempting to restore an antique radio, be sure to take the necessary precautionary steps to protect yourself and your work environment. Work out in an open, well-ventilated area or use an appropriate fume hood. Wear a face mask or respirator when necessary, especially when dealing with components that are prone to release hazardous particles or fumes. Wear safety goggles or glasses that provide ample protection from flying shards of glass and other objects.

Discharge Equipment

It is essential to ensure that any equipment you are working on is properly discharged. This is often overlooked, especially when dealing with older vintage units that do not contain protective mechanisms. If you come into contact with any electrical components, be sure to use a suitable voltmeter to check for voltage and to discharge any capacitors correctly.

Wear Eye Protection

Eye protection is a must when working on any type of vintage unit. Not only can the flashes from power switches or the sparks from soldering irons be damaging to your eyes, but they can also be a sign of a fault or good conductor. Make sure to wear appropriate safety glasses when working with any type of device. Best practice when repairing a vintage unit is to completely remove the cabinet and all related components. This way you can examine the circuitry and wiring properly, as well as check for any damaged components. Be careful when handling any wiring or moving parts, as these can become worn out over time and can be a safety hazard. Before tackling any repairs, be sure to take note of the wiring diagram or schematics to ensure that all connections are secure and safe.

To restore an antique radio correctly and safely, it is important to become familiar with the device and the various components inside it. While troubleshooting or repairing an antique radio, always be aware of live wires or components. Never touch the outside of components or wiring unnecessarily, as this could cause a deadly shock. If you must work on a live circuit, use a GFCI outlet or some other method of overload protection. If a shock occurs, immediately turn off the power and assess the damage. When restoring an antique radio to its full potential, it is important to take safety into account. From protective gear to proper discharge of components and information of the device's circuitry, your safety and the safety of your vintage unit should be considered. With the proper precautions and a bit of experience, you can expertly restore any antique radio back to life.

Chapter 4: Radio Design Basics

The area of radio design is a fascinating one, as it takes many different forms and has a long history. In this chapter, we'll explore the basics of radio design that each restorer should understand. We'll look at the three main components of any radio design, namely transistors, vacuum tubes, and tuning circuits, as well as frequency control elements.

Transistors

Transistors are the essential component of any modern radio design. They are small, relatively inexpensive devices that regulate current and form the basis of digital circuitry. Transistors consist of three terminals called the base, collector, and emitter. A current runs from the base to the collector and from the collector to the emitter. The flow of current is controlled by the base current, and the transistor is used to switch signals on or off. Transistor radios generally used a single transistor for the entire radio and relied on the transistor to process signals directly. This meant that the signals had to be filtered through a circuit before they could be broadcast. Modern radios use integrated circuits with many transistors on them to process multiple signals simultaneously.

Vacuum Tubes

Vacuum tubes were the earliest form of radio design and were used in most radios prior to the introduction of transistors. A vacuum tube consists of a glass tube with electrodes placed inside. By heating them, electrons in the air can be drawn off to form a current. Vacuum tubes are very efficient at amplifying signals, but they draw a lot of power. Because of this, vacuum tube radios were often much larger than those that used transistors. The vacuum tubes in a radio could also easily become damaged, making the radio unusable until the tubes were replaced.

Tuning Circuits

Tuning circuits are essential to a radio design because they allow the radio to receive signals across a range of different frequencies. A tuning circuit consists of a capacitor and inductor arranged in series or parallel. The capacitor stores energy so that when it is exposed to a radio signal, it can react by allowing only the desired frequencies to pass through. Tuning circuits are used to determine the types of frequencies that can be received by the radio and are usually tuned to match the station frequencies available in the area. The tuning range of the circuit is determined by the size of the inductor and capacitor and by the type of material used in the circuit.

Frequency Control Elements

Frequency control elements are necessary in any radio since they allow the user to control the exact frequency of the radio. This is done by adjusting the capacitance or inductance of the circuit. Frequency control elements can be manual or can be controlled electronically by a microcontroller. Manual frequency control elements consist of a knob or switch that adjusts the capacitance or inductance of the circuit. Electronic frequency control elements use small capacitors or inductors that can be precisely adjusted by a microcontroller. In conclusion, radio design is a complex and interesting field. Understanding the basics of each element of a radio design is essential in order for a restorer to be successful in their work. With all of these core components, any restorer can create a radio that is capable of functioning just as well – if not better – than the original.

Chapter 5: Testing Procedures

Testing Routine

When conducting testing procedures on an antique radio, it is important to take a systematic approach. First, take a few moments to examine the radio's exterior: visually inspect any exposed components, look for signs of corrosion, and clean the radio of any dirt or grime that has accumulated over time. Even if the radio appears to be in good condition, it is best to open up the device and examine the internals. Open any plugged components, like the speaker, and check the interior of the radio for defective capacitors and other worn-out parts. It is also important to plug the radio into a power source and test for power. This can be done easily with a voltmeter set to measure DC voltage.

Connect the voltmeter to the power cord, plug it in, and take a reading. The reading should match the correct supply voltage for the component. After the initial inspection, an electrical test should be performed. Begin by testing the switches, buttons, and other controls to make sure they are in proper working order. To check for any shorts, use an ohmmeter. Additionally, electronic components like capacitors and resistors must be tested with a capacitance and resistance meter, respectively. Once all of the component parts have been tested, the radio's circuit should be checked. This should be done with a schematic diagram of the component in hand. By tracing the component's circuit, any problems with the device's wiring can be identified.

Results Analysis

Once all the tests are complete, the results should be analyzed. First, go through the component parts and take note of any that are not working properly. If a component cannot be repaired, it should be replaced with an equivalent component. It is important to remember that when replacing components in an antique radio, the component should be as close to the original part as possible in order to preserve the historical integrity of the device. Once the component parts have been addressed, examine the electrical testing results. If all is well, reassemble the component. If, on the other hand, the electrical tests got different results than what were expected, there are a few common problems that could be the cause. These include faulty contacts, shorted transformers, and open circuits. All of these should be addressed with a common set of troubleshooting procedures.

Reports and Documentation

Once the antique radio has been restored, it is time to document the project and the results. Detailed reports should be written for each component and all issues that were encountered during the repairs.

These reports should include detailed information about the original condition of the component, the issues that were fixed, and any parts that were replaced. The reports should also include photographs, wiring diagrams and schematics, and any other important information that could be helpful in the future. Finally, keep detailed records of the repair. This will be especially helpful if the radio needs to be serviced at a later date. Good record keeping will eliminate having to start the process from scratch.

Taking the time to document the repairs can save time and frustration down the road when the service is needed. Documenting the repairs can also provide the opportunity to showcase the restoration process. Keeping photographs of the original radio and of all of the components being replaced can provide a nice before-and-after story that can be shared with future generations. Even more impressive is the knowledge that the service was conducted in such a way that preserves the historical integrity of the antique radio.

Chapter 6: Component Replacement

Restoring antique radios is a labor of love; it requires an abundance of patience, enthusiasm and technical skill. In this chapter, we will discuss the key concepts of component replacement in an antique radio circuit. Often, repairing or replacing basic components can be a great way to restore an antique radio.

Removing and Replacing Electrical Components

Removing and replacing components can be tricky. You will need to be cautious as you take careful measurements of the components to be removed and the components you plan to replace them with. This will be especially important for components such as transformer windings, capacitors and switches that are hardwired into the circuit. You should also make sure to clearly mark each of the components before starting the disassembly process, so that it's easier to reassemble the radio. When removing electrical components, it's also important to be generous with the use of flux paste (a flux paste is a paste-like substance used in soldering). This can help to ensure that all the solder points hold and that you don't run into any problems when putting the new components in place. Additionally, it's a good idea to clean each joint before beginning the process of soldering. A homemade mixture of rubbing alcohol and vinegar can help to eradicate the joint prior to heat.

Replacing Paper and Wax Resistors

Paper and wax resistors are usually found in antique radios and will usually need to be replaced over the course of a restoration. There are a few things to consider when replacing these resistors, such as the value of the replacement (it should be the same as the original resistor) and the power rating as well (it should also match the rating of the original resistor). When soldering, you should use the same techniques and precautions that you would with any other component. Always make sure to use some flux paste and clean the joint before adding heat. Also, always heat the joint from the bottom up, which will help to ensure that the solder flows evenly and easily. In addition to soldering, you may need to use some kind of mechanical device like tweezers to carefully extract the old resistor. If the resistor is glued in place, you may need to gently pry it out with a flat-headed screwdriver. It's important to be gentle with these components, since they can be quite delicate and break easily. If the value of the original resistor that you are replacing is not printed on the resistor, you will need to take measures to seek out its value. You can do this by using an ohmmeter to test its resistance value. You should also make sure that the resistance value of the new resistor is within tolerance of the original value of the resistor being replaced (this is usually indicated on the resistor).

Once you have identified the correct value for the replacement resistor, you will be able to fit it into the circuit and continue without any problems. If a resistor is damaged or too far out of tolerance, you may need to consider replacing it with another of the same value, but with a slightly higher wattage rating. This concludes the discussion of component replacement in an antique radio. When replacing components, it's important to take careful measurements and handle them with care. In addition to measuring the components, it's also important to use flux paste and clean the joints before soldering. Finally, it's important to make sure the replacement value and wattage of the components match that of the original. Careful attention to these details can help to ensure the repair process goes smoothly, and your antique radio will be up and running in no time!

Replacing and Cleaning Pots, Volume Knobs and Switches

When replacing pots, volume knobs and switches, it's important to know how to do it safely and correctly. To start off, begin by straightening bent terminals, and then use a small, flat screwdriver to get underneath the component and twist it off, being careful not to damage the circuit board. Before you place the new component, clean the area where the old component was. This will prevent any dust or other impurities from preventing a good circuit connection. When looking for a new component, you have a few choices of material. Carbon-based potentiometers are the most common, and preferred by many. These are usually the cheapest, which makes them a great choice for restoration projects.

Metal-based components are often preferable for high-end audio applications, for the added performance and durability, but usually come with more of a price tag. Each material has its pros and cons, so deciding which one to go with depends on the job at hand. The next step is to clean up the component itself before installing it. Both carbon and metal components can be cleaned using a cleaning agent such as contact cleaner or deoxidant. For plastic components, you may want to use a small brush or toothpick to get rid of any dust and dirt. Just be careful not to use any harsh chemicals, as the plastic can crack or melt. Now, when it comes to installing the component, make sure to line up the pins properly before pressing down firmly. Once the component is installed, make sure to secure the pot, knob or switch with the necessary mounting screws.

To finish off, make sure to check for any loose wires or damaged terminals. It is much easier to diagnose and fix a loose connection before the radio is in use, rather than after it's switched on.

Polishing

After replacing any components, the radio should look fresh and new. Unfortunately, many of these pieces become dull, scratched or generally worn down over time. Without properly polishing these components, the radio won't look as clean and crisp as you'd like. To start, use a soft cloth to apply a mild cleaner and polish. A wide variety of polish exists, and using the wrong one can damage the materials. For plastic knobs, a mild cleaner is perfectly acceptable. For metal components, use a polish that contains carnauba wax. This will help bring back the glossy shine. For dial indicators and switches, a separate special brush may be necessary to remove the built up grime. To finish off, give them a good clean with a soft cloth and polish where necessary.

It's also important to note that it may not be possible to restore the restored components to their former glory, especially if they are significantly worn down. In cases like these, it may be worthwhile to find replacement components, at least for the more visible parts such as the dial indicator and volume knob. In any case, a sturdy, clean and polished radio should be the result of some careful cleaning, polishing and if necessary, replacing knobs, indicators and switches. With some patience and elbow grease, each piece can be restored to its former glory, leaving your radio looking as good as new.

Chapter 7: Tools of the Trade

Today's restoration projects are very different from those from the early days of radio. A wide array of tools is necessary to get the job done. From soldering irons to sophisticated diagnostic tools, getting the right tools for the task can make all of the difference in the success of your project.

Soldering Irons

The soldering iron is probably the most important tool in the restorer's arsenal. When installing replacement components, soldering is the only reasonable option. As metals and plastics have become more sophisticated, so too have the soldering irons available to the restorer. Today, there are several different types of soldering irons available. The most popular and economical form is the manually-adjustable model. This type of solderer has an adjustable dial that allows the user to select the desired temperature.

This is a good choice for most applications and is usually adequate for smaller repair jobs. A slightly more expensive option is an automatically-adjusting model. These are becoming more popular with professional restorers and require minimal user intervention when soldering components. They will automatically adjust the plate temperature to the correct setting for the job being performed. Another type of soldering iron is the hand-held variety. These are becoming increasingly popular with those tackling more advanced projects, such as restoring antique radios. These are relatively easy to use, are quite versatile, and require only one hand operation.

Desoldering Tools

To remove components from a printed circuit board, a more specialized tool is needed. These are called desoldering tools and are typically of two types. The first type is a simple vacuum pump. This is inserted into the pads of a component and, when activated, will suck up all of the excess solder from the board. This is a relatively simple process and is usually adequate for most projects. The second type of desoldering tool is called a hot-air desoldering gun. This is a specialized device that uses a heated nozzle to remove solder without damaging the underlying components. This is the preferred method for more intricate and delicate jobs, such as those found within antique radios.

Testing Equipment

Most restorers need reliable test equipment in order to diagnose problems within their projects. The most basic and essential piece of this equipment is a multimeter. This is a compact device that can measure voltage, current, and resistance. This is essential for determining short circuits and verifying that a particular component is still functioning. More advanced testing equipment, such as waveform generators and signal sources, can provide more detailed information. These are particularly useful when trying to diagnose the exact cause of a problem or when attempting to tune a radio for optimum performance.

Diagnostic Tools

Modern diagnostic tools have revolutionized the way restorers troubleshoot and repair their projects. These tools can range from the relatively simple to the very complex. The most basic of these is the diagnostic software package. This can be used to analyze the functions of a particular device, such as a transistor or an integrated circuit. Some packages will even generate a printout of the results, which can be used to quickly identify and isolate the main cause of a problem. More advanced diagnostic tools, such as oscilloscopes and logic analyzers, can provide detailed information about the inner workings of a device. These are often used to pinpoint the precise cause of a problem and can be invaluable when attempting to repair electronic components. Restoring antique radios can be an incredibly rewarding endeavor. However, it is important to be equipped with the proper tools for the job. Don't skimp on quality, or you may find yourself unable to complete a project. Soldering irons, desoldering tools, testing equipment, and diagnostic tools are just some of the tools required by the modern radio restorer, and having the right ones for the job can make all the difference.

Chapter 8: Interpreting Documentation

The array of instructions, diagrams, schematics, illustrations and parts lists that accompany the restoration of old radios can sometimes seem dizzying. While it's not enough to simply observe these documents, it is invaluable to be able to interpret them correctly in order to determine the effects of certain modifications and repairs. This chapter will provide a thorough overview of the importance of documentation for antique radio restoration, as well as practical tips for understanding and applying the information.

Locating and Analyzing Service Manuals

The starting point for navigating the complex network of documents associated with antique radios is to locate service manuals or schematic diagrams. In some cases, it may take some research through online archives or the use of specialized books to uncover diagrams; however, with some radios, such as those produced after 1962, manufacturers usually created some form of comprehensive manual. When consulting a service manual, it's crucial to go beyond the most basic information it provides. It's essential to also consider the implications of certain elements, such as the electrical design, to accurately determine the cause of an issue and its solution. In other words, it's not enough to simply be able to read the numbers and letters, but rather to be able to think logically and analytically about the implications of certain design decisions. A thorough understanding of components, circuitry and connections can also be helpful.

Operating Instructions

Antique radio restoration usually requires at least some operating instructions to be consulted in order to properly set up and operate the machines. Manuals and diagrams sometimes bundled together with the radio can sometimes offer detailed information on tuning, amplifying, and more; however, it's not always possible to find such documents. In this case, some experimentation with the radio is sometimes necessary. In order to make sense of the instructions it's important to closely review the radio and its components. It's crucial to become familiar with the various components, such as volume controls and tuning knobs, and the effects of making adjustments or modifications. Understanding circuitry is also helpful: Paying close attention to the design of the amplifier, for example, can provide valuable insight into its operation. When studying both service manuals and operating instructions, some research into the design of common radio components, such as tubes and resistors, is necessary.

Knowledge of elements such as load impedance, cut-off frequency, and frequency response is necessary to properly interpret vintage schematics and make sense of the instructions. This additional understanding can also assist in making modifications, such as re-capping, in order to optimize a radio's performance. Though some of the documents associated with antique radio restoration may seem daunting at first, it's certainly possible to make sense of them with a bit of research and creative thinking. With a careful eye and a thorough understanding of the various components that make up a vintage radio, it's possible to turn a jumble of words and numbers into a comprehensive plan of action. Clinging to the basics, paying attention to details and examining schematics can assist even the most amateur of restorers. As with any endeavor, practice makes perfect when dealing with the documentation associated with antique radio restoration. With enough exploration, interpretation and experimentation, the task of properly restoring aging radios could become a breeze.

Chapter 9: Best Practices for Handling and Storing Parts

Restoring an antique radio requires many delicate parts, and a more experienced technician will understand the importance of protecting their quality and performance. With so many components at the ready, it can be difficult to keep them properly labeled and organized. This chapter will provide detailed guidance on the best practices for handling and storing parts to ensure efficient, error-free restoration.

Managing Stock

The first step of efficient and safe part storage is to keep track of all the various components. It's easy to get lost in a mechanic's workshop, especially when the inventory is constantly changing. To avoid this, it's a good idea to label each box of components and ensure they can be identified at a glance. This will make the job of locating a specific part or type of part much easier and quicker. Additionally, and just as important, a simple inventory management system should be put in place so that it's easy to tell when components are running low or when parts must be re-ordered.

Labeling Parts

Another important practice when handling and storing parts for an antique radio is proper labeling. This should not be done just for the sake of neatness, but it should also be used to provide clarity. Each part and its location should be clearly labeled and easy to find. This includes labeling the components on the radio itself. Without properly labeled parts, it can be difficult to remember what and where parts have been replaced or adjusted. Furthermore, in the event that a part must be exchanged, a well-presented label can save a great deal of time and frustration.

Cleaning Components

Whenever possible, when handling and storing antique radio parts, it is important to clean and lubricate them if necessary. This is particularly important for moving parts, such as motors and relays, but also for contact points, such as connectors and switches. Over time, dust and dirt can build up on electrical contacts, reducing performance and even causing short circuits. Cleaning these parts with a soft cloth and contact-safe cleaners is an essential process to improve radio performance and reliability. In addition, it is also important to lubricate moving parts in order to protect them against wear and tear. Even when components are not visibly dirty, lubrication can help protect against the slow deterioration of the delicate parts that are so vital to a successful restoration. By following these best practices, it is much easier to ensure that the components required to restore an antique radio remain in perfect condition. With properly labeled and clean parts, an experienced technician can ensure that restoration work is completed quickly and efficiently.

Chapter 10: Disassembling and Assessing

For those looking to carry out antique radio restoration, ensuring proper disassembly and assessment of the device is essential to success. The process of restoring, repairing, and modernizing an old or rare model of a radio can be a deceptively complex and time-consuming task, and without proper preparation and due diligence prior to starting work, even the most carefully laid plans can quickly become derailed by unexpected setbacks caused by various imperfections, faults, or miscellaneous issues. Knowledge is power, so let's take a look at the art of disassembling and assessing antique radios, so that the radio-restorer can properly plan for each stage of the restoration process.

Dismantling the Radio

This initial and most essential step of the process is when the radio is opened up, taking apart its many layers to reveal the inner workings and components. This requires special care and precision, as even the most minuscule details can make all the difference as to how the project progresses; any potential damage caused at this stage can not only lead to additional costs and repairs, it can result in long-term impacts on the radio's performance, once completed. It is recommended to use an "exploded view" diagram of the model in question, as these provide an invaluable resource to guide the restorer step-by-step through the process.

As much as possible, it is important to retain a level of organization throughout the process, and that's why it's essential to label all components, as well as place them in order as they are taken apart. Once the radio is fully taken apart, the next step is to take a closer look at each individual part. All parts should be personally inspected and assessed in order to ensure that they are fit for work, match the device's specific requirements, and identify any potential replacements or upgrades. Taking pictures of all parts is an essential method for keeping accurate records for reference, and making sure that nothing gets mixed up during the process.

Assessing to Determine Scope of Work

Once a thorough review of the components is complete, the next step is to assess the overall condition of the components and how they will perform after the restoration is completed. Taking a close look at the overall performance of the device and its individual parts requires knowledge, understanding, and foresight on the part of the restorer; the experienced pro will be able to spot potential problems and not tried solutions by simply inspecting the organ, knobs, switches and wires. The next step is to create a detailed inventory list, which should include all components required for the particular radio. This should include not only standard radio parts, but also more obscure pieces that may be difficult to find. For example, vintage brass connectors, tuning dial mechanisms, and spare parts from the manufacturer of the peculiar model in question.

Having a precise inventory list is essential for planning and estimating the time and costs of the project as a whole. Once you have gathered all the necessary components and assessed their condition, you are ready to continue with your restoration project! By taking the time to properly evaluate the project's requirements and create a comprehensive list of parts, you will be able to make the right decisions in terms of time and efficiency, helping you get the most bang for your buck during the radio restoration process.

Chapter 11: Restoring Wood Cabinets and Knobs

The intricate beauty of antique radios can often be found in the materials used to craft its cabinets and knobs. For many collectors, this is the area that will require the most delicate attention, as restoring wood can easily involve more risks than benefits. Fortunately, with the right materials and the right approach, vintage wood radio cabinets and knobs can be brought back to life without causing any damage to the original piece.

Raw Materials

Before even considering restoring a wooden radio cabinet or knob, a few raw materials must be obtained. Depending on the project, some of these items might include wood glue, saws, sandpaper, wood putty, wood finishes, and polishing cloths. Additionally, it's important to keep a few tips in mind when shopping for materials for any woodworking job. Primarily, the item should be measured correctly, as it should not be bigger or smaller than the original piece. Secondly, the color should match -- even when it comes to constructing or restoring a knob or cabinet, there are few things more aesthetically displeasing than mismatched colors. Last, the materials should be safe for use -- any toxic substances should be avoided at all costs.

Finishing Materials

Once the raw materials have been obtained, the restoration or construction process can begin. Depending on the piece, this may require specific finishing materials such as shellacs, varnishes, and polishes. The type of finishing material used depends on the item -- for example, shellac is generally used for more delicate pieces such as buttons, while varnishing may be required for more robust items, such as furniture. When choosing a finishing material, it is important to select a type that is safe for use on wood, as well as a color that matches the original piece.

Process Overview

As previously stated, each restoration project is different and often requires slightly different approaches. However, the overall process can be divided into a few distinct steps which should be followed regardless of the item. The first step is to take detailed measurements of the item to be restored or constructed, so that the correct materials can be obtained. Secondly, the item should be stripped of any previous finishes, and all old paint or varnish should be removed. Finally, the newly obtained materials can then be used to properly restore the wood back to its original state. When restoring a radio cabinet, the most important step is to ensure the materials are matched to the original cabinet. Restoring the item will involve cleaning and sanding, as well as filling in any defects or cracks with wood putty.

The piece should then be stained and varnished to match the original color of the cabinet, before it is finally polished. In some cases, it might also be necessary to use a hand-held router to create any intricate details that may have been lost to the years. Similarly, for restoring knobs, it will be important to ensure accuracy in the selection and placement of new materials. Depending on the type of knob, the process can involve hollowing out the existing knob before filling in the new material. This may then need to be sanded and shaped before it can be stained and polished. After the new material is in place, the knob can then be screwed back onto the radio and the process is complete. Of course, as a more general caution, it's important to remember that woodworking is a very delicate art form and should only be attempted by those with a good amount of experience.

Amateur woodworking can result in irreversible damage to the radio, the cabinet, or even leave the collector open to potential lawsuits. Before undertaking any restoration project, it is important to receive the proper training and advice in order to avoid any costly mistakes. Whether it's restoring an old radio cabinet or constructing a new knob, the process of bringing a piece of vintage wood back to life can be a delicate undertaking. With the right materials and the correct approach, however, these antique pieces can be restored and enjoyed by collectors for years to come.

Chapter 12: Wiring the Attic Antique

The task of wiring an antique radio takes some patience and skill, as well as knowledge of how the device was designed. Working on an attic antique can be a real challenge as most of these radios are more than half a century old and they can be quite fragile. But with a little bit of patience and by following certain guidelines, any antique radio enthusiast can successfully unravel the mystery of these attic antiques.

Removing and Replacing Bad Wiring

The first step in wiring an attic antique is to inspect the existing wiring for signs of wear and tear. Visible signs such as separated insulation, loose connections, cracked insulation, frayed wiring, and exposed wires should all be replaced. Wires that are especially fragile should be gently taken apart from their connections, as gently sliding a knife along the insulation can help reduce the amount of damage to the insulation. Once all of the old wiring has been removed, the connections should be well-cleaned using a cotton swab or a soft brush to ensure that all strands of the old wiring are removed.

The next step is to decide which type of connection should be used. Generally, it is best to avoid soldering when wiring an attic antique as solder can easily ruin components. Instead, it is best to use crimp connections, butt-splice terminals, or braided adhesive tape. Crimp connections are the best choice when joining shielded cables together, as they provide a secure connection that will not loosen over time. Using butt-splice terminals is also a good option if the wires need to be fastened securely together. Finally, braided adhesive tape can be used to insulate the connections and prevent any potential short circuits.

Lugging Connections

Lugging connections are an integral part of wiring an attic antique, as they provide a secure connection between cables and components. Lugging is basically an electrical connection which is made using a special lug connector. Generally, this type of connection is used when connecting components to a shielded cable, as it helps to reduce the chance of interference between different components. When lugging wires to a component, it is important to make sure that the wires are correctly inserted and that a tight connection is made. To ensure a secure connection, it is necessary to ensure that the wires are correctly tightened using a pair of pliers or a special lugging tool.

Agraffes

Agraffes are a type of connection commonly used in vintage radios, and they provide a secure connection between different components. This type of connection is made by soldering a threaded rod or nut to each component, then attaching them together with nuts and bolts. Agraffes provide a secure and reliable connection between components, and it is also possible to insulate the wires between them for additional protection. Ultimately, agraffes are a reliable and secure way to join different components in an attic antique. When wiring an attic antique, it is always important to remember to treat each component with the utmost care and respect. Antique radios should be handled with the utmost care and caution, as components can easily become damaged by mishandling. Additionally, exercising patience and taking the time to make sure all connections are properly made is a key component of ensuring a successful restoration. Following these steps can help to ensure that any attic antique can be brought back to life and experienced once again.

Chapter 13: Soldering

Soldering is an important skill to master when it comes to antique radio restoration. It requires precision and patience to achieve proper results. In this chapter, we will discuss the proper temperature settings, wire soldering, and gently removing old connections.

Proper Temperature Settings

The first step of soldering correctly is to ensure the correct and stable soldering temperature. Generally speaking, 400°F (204° C) is usually the best temperature to begin with. This temperature should be regulated and maintained constantly and without ever exceeding 500°F (260°C). The temperature can affect the performance of the radio much like how old circuits and components can. Too high a temperature can damage or even melt components and connections. A soldering station with a digitally regulated temperature setting is the best choice. This way, you can precisely set the temperature to the exact rate you need. There are also different types of soldering irons, such as a pencil soldering iron which is ideal for intricate wiring and repairs. The wattage should be appropriate for the amount and type of work being done. Start with a 40 Watt iron and then switch to a higher wattage as needed. An important point to keep in mind is to never use too much heat when soldering. It is always best to use the minimum amount of heat required to get the job done. Overheating can cause damage to the components and connections you are trying to repair.

Wire Soldering

Wire soldering is another important aspect to successfully complete antique radio restoration. To prepare your wires for soldering, use wire strippers or scissors to strip away the insulation. Then, depending on the conditions of the wire, you can use an abrasive paper to make it smooth to ensure an even solder flow. When actually soldering, you need to ensure that all pieces are clean and free from debris, dirt or rust. You can use a scrubbing pad or a damp cloth to clean the surfaces. When applying the solder, use the minimum amount required to ensure proper electrical contact with the two surfaces. You need to then let the assembled parts cool completely before handling. Avoid shock or movement of the joined pieces as this can cause a bad electrical contact. Make sure that you inspect all the points where the wire and connection have been soldered and repairs as necessary.

Gently Removing Old Connections

Sometimes in antique radio restoration, you will need to remove old connections such as pipes and brackets. The trick is to not use too much force and to be gentle. Use a sharp tool such as a screwdriver to carefully pry off the pieces, focusing on one side at a time. Always protect the parts with a piece of wood or a cushion so that the force is not focused on the part you are trying to protect. You can also use a soldering iron to heat up the joint and to soften the solder so that it can be taken apart more easily. If the connection is stubborn, you may have to use some fabrication tools such as a hammer and chisel to break it apart. If the connection has a slot that can fit a hacksaw blade, you can use it as an advantage to gently saw it off and then work on the remains to further loosen the parts.

Use a pair of pliers to hold the parts with and provide more leverage to gently pull the two pieces apart. Whatever tool you choose, it's important to take your time, apply minimal pressure and to not damage the fragile parts. When it comes to successfully restoring an antique radio, the repair process is a delicate and precise one, requiring patience and precision. With the proper temperature settings, wire soldering and gentle removal of old connections, you should be able to restore your radio to work as it once did.

Chapter 14: Installing Tubes and Resistors

Restoring antique radios requires a great deal of skill and patience, as many components can be decades or even centuries old, rendering them fragile and difficult to work with. One of the most fundamental steps involved in antique radio restoration is installing tubes and resistors. In this chapter, we will cover a few of the best practices for installing these components and explain their importance in the success of a radio restoration.

Installing Cooling Fan

When restoring antique radios, it is essential to consider the effects of heat when installing components. This is especially important with vacuum tubes, which can easily become too hot and malfunction if not properly ventilated. A cooling fan can help to ensure that the tubes are kept at a safe temperature and prolong the life of the unit. To install a cooling fan, locate an appropriate opening in the faceplate or cabinet of the radio, then attach the fan with screws or metal tape. Make sure to align the fan correctly so that the airflow is directed at the tubes, and use appropriate grommets or foam to keep the fan from rattling against the cabinet.

Replacing Old Second-hand Tubes

When replacing old, second-hand tubes, it is important to ensure that the new tube is of the same type and rating as the old one. Radio vintage must be taken into consideration as well, since some tubes may be incompatible with newer radios. To replace the old tube, carefully remove it from its socket with a pair of tweezers and insert the new tube. Make sure to check the polarity of the tube before inserting it into the socket, to avoid damaging either the tube or the socket.

Resistance Values

When replacing components, it is essential to make sure that their resistance values are as close to the original values as possible. This is especially crucial for resistors, which can quickly become too hot and malfunction if their resistance is too high. To avoid this, use an ohm meter to check the resistance of the new resistor before installing it. If necessary, use a resistor substitution box to choose resistors with the correct values. In addition, it is important to check the resistance of the surrounding components when installing a new resistor, to make sure that the resistance of the circuit as a whole is not compromised. This is especially important when dealing with power supplies, as incorrect resistance values can lead to dangerous overloads and shorts. Finally, when installing resistors, make sure to use the appropriate type of resistor for the circuit.

Some circuits may require wire-wound resistors, which are able to handle higher wattage and better accuracy than standard carbon-film resistors. Installing tubes and resistors is an important step in finishing any antique radio restoration project. By following the best practices outlined here, you can ensure that your project is a success. Remember to research the specifics of each component before starting the installation process, and always double check the resistance values of all components to avoid potential overloads and shorts.

Chapter 15: Re-capping

The process of re-capping antique radios is a necessary step for many restoration projects. Re-capping – or replacing the capacitors – helps ensure the integrity of a vintage radio, and also helps improve sound quality. To begin a re-capping job, the process begins by carefully removing the chassis from the cabinet and taking out the tubes. Tubes are delicate and should be handled with extreme caution. It's important to note that the voltage is still present after taking out the tubes, so all re-capping must take place in an electrically insulated environment.

Replacing Capacitors

The actual process of replacing the capacitors is relatively straightforward. Most capacitors are quite easy to identify and remove. First, locate and record the original capacitors before removing them, noting their position and connections. This allows the new capacitors to be installed correctly. Having done this, disconnect the capacitors, making sure not to accidentally remove any others at the same time, and replace each one with the new capacitor. Note that different types of capacitor require different treatments for removal. Some may require more insulation, and larger, bulky devices may require moving other components first.

Observing Polarity

When removing the original device, take a good look at it and pay attention to the polarity markings (the arrow) as this will help when installing the new capacitor. Note also that there can be two entirely different devices with the same value, so be sure to get the right one. Another important aspect of capacitor removal and replacement is the color-coding. Every capacitor should have a color or number that indicates its value, so make sure to double-check this before attaching it.

Rerouting Power

When replacing the capacitors, it's important to reroute the power supply wires if necessary. This process is simpler than it might sound – once you have identified the wires, it's just a matter of joining them all up correctly. Be careful to avoid any overheating of components, and it is often a good idea to isolate the supply wires using electrical tape. The process of re-capping an antique radio can be satisfying, but it is essential to take the necessary safety precautions and exercise caution throughout. Replacing the capacitors correctly is a great way to ensure the safety and performance of antique radios, and most vintage radio enthusiasts make it part of their regular maintenance schedule. Have fun and work carefully, and you will be rewarded with a restored vintage radio that will provide many hours of music and pleasure for years to come.

Chapter 16: Re-Aligning the Radio

Maintaining the performance of an antique radio is a lifelong process. If a collector has the resources, they may choose to have the radio re-aligned on a regular basis. This process can be both simple and complex, depending on the type of radio and the degree of customization that is needed. Realignment is a key factor in keeping any radio performance-ready and up to date. It should be noted that this is an advanced procedure and should not be undertaken without the appropriate technical assistance.

Calibration and Re-Alignment

Calibration and re-alignment are two related but separate processes that allow for the optimization of a radio to ensure its best performance. The main goal of calibration is to bring the radio back into factory specifications and make sure it is performing per the manufacturer's design. During a re-alignment, the collector has the ability to adjust the output to the best of its capabilities and make other customizations per their own unique specifications. Calibrating a radio involves a number of steps, such as tuning the electrodes and high-frequency oscillators as well as scheduling adjustments for the filters and resonators. In addition to ensuring that the radio is operating at its peak performance, calibration also helps minimize noise and other unwanted sounds that can be emitted from an untuned-radio. Re-aligning a radio involves adjusting a wide range of components to produce the desired sound quality. Adjustments are performed on the antenna tuning system, IF transformers and the detector or receiver.

This process also includes changing the bias and grid setting to improve the functioning of the radio's circuitry. Lastly, the collector can make adjustments to the audio system and refine the tuning of the modulation and selectivity circuits for a more accurate sound.

Adjusting for Spectrum Balance

Spectrum balance is an important element of displaying broadcasted audio accurately on a radio. It is a process of obtaining peak performance from audio frequencies. To begin, a radio will be tested at predetermined frequencies and adjustments made as necessary to equalize the gain or volume levels throughout the frequency range. The alignment of the radio's circuit components must be precise in order to achieve the desired sound quality. Spectrum balance should also include changing the antenna and oscillator adjustments as well as compensating for sub-tone issues that can be caused by an unbalanced spectrum. The distortion of sound due to a skewed spectrum can be minimized by making sure that all of the components are calibrated for each band of frequencies. In addition, tweaks can be made to the grid and filament bias to enhance the overall tone of the radio.

Accurately adjusting the spectrum balance on a vintage AM/FM radio is a time-consuming as well as a delicate task. The best results are achieved by using the appropriate tools and precision instruments, such as capacitance and leakage meters. By paying close attention to the details and following a proven methodology, an experienced collector can realign their antique radio to meet the demands of modern broadcasting technology, ensuring that their piece of history will be enjoyed for many years to come.

Chapter 17: Final Touches

When it comes to antique radio restoration, the final touches are one of the most critical aspects of the project. After all, a well-restored radio should look every bit as beautiful and professional as it did when it left the assembly line. To ensure the highest level of quality, no detail should be overlooked in the restoration process. This chapter will provide an overview of the best practices for ensuring a top-quality restoration.

Cleaning

Cleaning the outside and inside of a vintage radio is essential for a quality restoration. It is important to polish off any dirt and grime from the exterior surfaces, as well as from inside the cabinet, knobs, and chassis. A mild cleaner such as rubbing alcohol is a great option for many materials, while brass and metal components will require specialty cleaners. It is also important to exercise caution when cleaning the exterior of the radio, as too much gardening can damage it or cause it to dull.

Final Tuning

In order to ensure that a beautifully restored vintage radio performs as it should, final tuning and adjustments should be completed. This includes fine-tuning the tuning ratio, aligning the RF coils and resonators, and adjusting the tracking, microphone gain, and tone controls. If the radio has an amplifier, it should be checked for any distortion, overshoot, and output at different frequencies and volumes levels.

Inspecting Connections

It is important to inspect all existing connections throughout the entire radio to ensure that they are secure and working properly. This includes inspecting the wires, connection blocks, and terminals for any sign of wear. If a connection is weakened or corroded, it should be replaced. Along with improving the performance of the radio, this also ensures that it is safe for operation.

Rejuvenating Motors

Vintage radio restoration often includes rejuvenating or replacing the motors. Motor brushes and bearings can wear over time and become inefficient or unresponsive. To improve the performance of a vintage radio, the brushes should be replaced and new bearings installed in order to reduce vibrations and friction. The motor should also be properly lubricated to help ensure optimal performance and a longer life. No matter the age, condition, or type of vintage radio being restored, the final touches are crucial for achieving a top-quality and professional restoration. From cleaning to tuning to inspecting connections and rejuvenating motors, every step should be done with the utmost care and attention. By taking the time to complete all of these steps, a radio can both look and perform like new.

Chapter 18: Final Performance Tests

Performance testing on an antique radio is a way of measuring the quality and accuracy of the restoration work done. It requires an understanding of the radio's technical specifications as a baseline and then comparing it to the actual performance of the restored radio. There are a variety of tests that can be used to determine the quality of the restoration, such as testing the radio's frequency response, signal-to-noise ratio, harmonic distortion, and bandpass accuracy. By understanding the different tests which can be used to measure performance, it is possible to accurately assess the success of the antique radio restoration.

Performance Measurements

The performance of an antique radio can be measured in a variety of ways, depending on the radio's functions and capabilities. Frequency response, signal-to-noise ratio, harmonic distortion and band pass accuracy are all tests which can be used to assess the quality of a restored radio. Frequency response measures the range of frequencies which the radio is able to transmit and receive, and is measured with an oscilloscope. The signal-to-noise ratio determines the amount of noise in the signal which can be heard, including any external sources of interference. Harmonic distortion determines the amount of distortion when the two signals are compared, while the bandpass accuracy tests how well the radio is able to accurately transmit and receive signals within its frequency range.

Enhancements

Once performance measurements have been taken, there are enhancements which may be required to bring the radio back up to professional standards. This can include returning and realignment of the front panel and receiver adjustments, as well as minor mechanical repairs. Additionally, it might also include the replacement of certain components such as old tubes and capacitors. These enhancements can help to improve the sound quality and performance of the radio and provide a more authentic experience for the listener.

Quality Control Protocols

The last step in the antique radio restoration process is the implementation of quality control protocols. This includes checking over the entire restoration project, including the components and the wiring of the radio. It also includes making sure all components and systems function as intended, and that the radio is performing to its best possible ability. It is important to follow a strict system of quality control protocols to ensure that the restoration is successful and that the final product is safe, reliable and accurate.

Chapter 19: Cleaning and Lubricating

Restoring an antique radio encompasses a variety of different tasks, but one of the most important of these is cleaning and lubricating the various parts and components. Not only does this ensure that the radio functions properly, but it also extends its lifespan and keeps it looking its best. In this chapter, we'll discuss the best practices for cleaning gears and galvanic cells, oiling motors and lubricating controls.

Cleaning Gears and Galvanic Cells

When it comes to cleaning gears in an antique radio, the best approach is to use a soft brush or cloth and a gentle cleaning solution, such as isopropyl alcohol. Avoid using harsh chemical cleaners, as these can cause corrosion and damage delicate components. For galvanic cells, the same rule applies. Carefully clean the cells using a softly bristled brush, or a cotton swab dampened in isopropyl alcohol.

Oiling Motors

The motors in antique radios require regular oiling in order to stay in proper working order. Depending on the type of motor, this can be done in one of a few ways. If the motor is an animating type (such as a vibrator), it will require a special oiling tool, which can be obtained from a specialty radio parts shop. The oil should be light and free of contaminants and should be applied sparingly. Be sure to wear protective gloves when handling oil, as it can be corrosive. For conventional motors, light oil, such as canola oil, can be added sparingly with a cotton swab. Once again, use proper caution when handling it.

Lubricating Controls and Switches

All of the switches, controls and knobs on the radio require lubrication in order to function properly. The best way to accomplish this is to apply a thin layer of high-quality, silicone-based lubricant to the components in question. Many specialist shops sell products specifically designed for use on antique radios; however, some experts advise using automotive brake grease or silicone oil, both of which can be found in hardware stores. Regardless of which product you choose, be sure to avoid any petroleum-based lubricants, as these can cause long-term damage to delicate components. In addition to lubricating all of the components, it's important to clean the various ports and connectors on the radio.

This can be done by carefully vacuuming the interior of the radio and wiping away any dust and debris. Be sure to use only a soft brush, as a stiff one can damage delicate components. The process of cleaning and lubricating an antique radio can be time-consuming and tedious, but it's an important part of the restoration process. Doing it properly will ensure that the radio runs smoothly and is ready to be enjoyed for years to come.

Chapter 20: A Deeper Look at Tuning Circuits

Antique radios are a fascinating hobby to collect and restore. Exploring the more mysterious aspects of radio circuits can give a sense of achievement and satisfaction. One aspect that can be a treasure trove of exploration is tuning circuits. Understanding the basics of such typically tunable components will give enthusiasts a great start in their journey of discovering the electronic intricacies that make these wonderful machines.

Understanding Frequency Control Elements

In order for an antique radio to tune in a range of different frequencies, many components are used to provide accuracy and exact tuning. One of the main frequency selection elements is the variable capacitor, also known as a trimmer capacitor. This is a variable capacitor on a fixed value capacitor to provide fine tuning of the radio frequency. In addition, variable resistors, known as variable inductance coils can also be used as another way to inductively tune the radio. When adjusted correctly, these components can provide the perfect frequency range. Adjusting these components can be tricky and often involves the use of specialized tools such as screwdrivers and wrenches. Being able to correctly adjust and replace these components can be a rewarding experience and allow for a wide range of skill improvement.

Tuning Capacitors

The tuning capabilities of an antique radio come from a variety of capacitors. These capacitors can range from standard fixed capacitors to variable capacitors. Each of these components serves a specific purpose. Fixed capacitors are used in antennas, while variable capacitors are used to fine-tune frequencies. The variable capacitor consists of two plates, known as the stator and rotor, that move back and forth in relation to one another. This movement then forms fluctuations in the capacitance of the capacitor and changes the frequency of the radio. These types of capacitors can also be used in combination with other components like inductors or resistors as part of a tuning circuit. Tuning capacitors can be quite delicate and require careful handling. It is important to ensure that the plates are not bent or damaged in any way. Furthermore, in some cases the capacitor may require lubrication to ensure smooth operation, as over time the plates can become stuck due to lack of use or age. By taking the time to experiment, restore and understand the intricate workings of a tuning circuit one can begin to appreciate the beauty that exists within a vintage radio.

As a result of this exploration, it is possible to gain in-depth knowledge of the basics of tuning that can be put to use when restoring antique radios and rescuing them from the brink of extinction.

Chapter 21: Testing with a Signal Source

When it comes to properly testing a tube or transistor radio, the use of a signal source is essential. A signal source is any device that can generate a range of frequencies. This may include a signal generator, radio receiver, or oscilloscope. Every radio needs to be tested in order to ensure its components are functioning as intended. This is also true for radios that may not be audible to the human ear. Let's take a look at the requirements of employing a signal source in the process of troubleshooting and testing a radio.

Signal Source Requirements

When using a signal source for testing radio components, the goal is for it to meld with the impedance (resistance to current) of the circuitry. This allows for the generated signal to be echoed back to the signal source at a frequency level or output amplitude. Depending on the type of signal source being used, the impedance should match that of the receiving circuit. Some sources are able to source a range of frequencies, while others are limited. Careful attention should be paid to the impedance to avoid damage to components or low-frequency response.

Utilizing a Signal Generator

To test oscillators and tuned circuits of a radio, a signal generator is the ideal tool to use. A signal generator can generate a wide range of frequencies, making it perfect for testing the components of a radio. This can be done by amplifying a generated signal and running it through the circuit. With the headphones on, if the radio is working properly, the generated signal will increase in amplitude when it hits the appropriate circuit frequency. If the signal decreases in amplitude, this may indicate an issue with the tuning components or the oscillator.

Employing Oscilloscope

Due to the frequency specific nature of testing a circuit with a signal source, the use of an oscilloscope may ease the process while increasing accuracy. Oscilloscopes display a waveform trace on a graph that can be measured to inspect its amplitude and frequency. This allows users to instantly detect and confirm issues in a circuit or with its components. An oscilloscope can also be used to examine the condition of transistors. This is particularly useful for detecting the gain value of an Audio Frequency Amplifier (AFX).

Testing a radio or its components can be an arduous task but with the use of a proper signal source, these tests will yield the information necessary to begin the repair process. While some testing can be done purely by ear, using a signal source like a signal generator or oscilloscope provides more data and accuracy. This allows users to pinpoint the problems in circuitry and be able to move forward with the proper steps to address them. In conclusion, the use of a signal source for testing radio components can greatly increase the efficiency of finding faults and repairing them. Signal sources offer a practical way of testing components without having to tear the radio apart and can provide key information about the condition of circuitry. Additionally, using a signal source to inspect components allows for frequency specific testing and can detect issues that traditional measurements cannot detect. Taking the time to utilize a signal source when repairing or restoring a radio can yield impressive results.

Chapter 22: Testing Radio Output

Radio technology has come a long way since the "Golden Age" of radio broadcasting. With today's modern electronics, it's easier than ever to test the output of a radio to figure out any problems that may be occurring. In order for a radio to broadcast properly, it needs to have its components accurately aligned, its resistance measures taken, and its power levels tested. In this chapter, we'll discuss all three of these processes, as well as how to identify any common problems that arise.

Alignment Requirements

It is important to align any radio properly in order to make sure that it is broadcasting accurately. There are several steps to the alignment process, and each one needs to be completed before proceeding to the next. It is best to begin with the antenna and RF amplifiers, as these need to be correctly adjusted to ensure that the signal is properly received. Then, the detector, amplifiers, and mixer all need to be adjusted for a consistent level. Finally, the speaker must be adjusted for a clear and even sound.

Resistance Checks

Before testing the output of the radio, it's important to check the radio circuitry for any problems. This should be done by measuring the resistance of each component, as this will help identify any resistance problems that may exist. Any resistance issues need to be identified and corrected in order to make sure that the radio is functioning properly. It is also important to make sure that the connections between components are secure, as a loose connection can cause the radio to fail.

Power Testing

The final step of the alignment process is to test the power levels. This can be done using an oscilloscope, as this will allow you to pinpoint any issues with the signal strength. Additionally, it can help identify potential overloads or any other power-related issues that may be causing the radio to fail. To ensure accuracy, it is important to remember that the oscilloscope should be set to an appropriate range when measuring power levels. Once the power levels have been measured, any issues can be addressed and corrected. Testing the output of a radio is a relatively simple process, and it doesn't require a lot of experience or special equipment.

Most of the steps are straightforward and can be completed by anyone with a basic understanding of radio technology. However, when dealing with antique radios it can be helpful to have a full understanding of the process and to check for any special requirements before getting started. Since the output of a radio is determined by its components and how they are connected, the condition of the components needs to be taken into consideration. For example, if a component is damaged or broken, then it needs to be replaced with a working one before any alignment can begin. Additionally, checking the wiring is also important, as any loose connections can lead to signal loss or distortion. It is also important to make sure that the ground connections are secure. Ground connections are necessary to ensure that the radio is properly grounded and that there is no interference with the signals being transmitted. Additionally, any stray signals need to be identified and dealt with so that their interference does not affect the quality of the signal. Overall, testing the output of a radio is an important part of keeping it running properly and for achieving clear and noise-free sound. By properly aligning, checking components, and testing the power levels, any radio can be tuned to its optimal performance level. With a little patience and understanding, you can ensure your radio operates at its best.

Chapter 23: Repairing Mechanical Components

Restoring antique radios can seem like a daunting task, especially for those new to the hobby. Though it may appear intimidating at first, restoring older radios involves many of the same skills as undertaking regular maintenance of current models. Much of the process is about understanding the components that make up the radio and learning how to assess and repair them. This chapter will focus on repairing the device's mechanical components, such as the tuners, bands, belts, spools, springs and clips.

Fixing Tuners and Bands

Tuners and bands are some of the components of a radio that require the most attention during repairs. Tuners are key to a radio's functionality, as topics are tuned in using these dials. It is also important to make sure that the information displayed on the face of each tuner is accurate - repair can involve replacing broken, worn, or out of sync dials. Tuners can be attached to their corresponding bands either by bolts, screws, or axles. It is important to check the integrity of these connections, as sagging bands can lead to distorted, unclear radio signals. Spring-tensioned bands must be carefully adjusted - if bands are too tight, for example, there is a risk of them being damaged when being tightened. It is therefore advisable to check all of the connections and adjust the spring-tensioned bands carefully.

Fixing Belts and Spools

Many antique radios rely on belts and spools to transmit and store power. The belt's tension should be monitored; if it is too tight, it can cause the spool to toil, instigating premature breakdown or damage. Similarly, if the belt is too loose, the spool will lose its connection to the belt and will no longer function properly. It is advisable to check the integrity of fan belts and spools during repairs, and to replace them if necessary. Where belts are concerned, the number of teeth, width, and circumference must match the corresponding spools. In most cases, it is not recommended to alter these measurements unless as a last resort. Belt-changing can be a time consuming process, as the alignment value must be set by hand. It is therefore recommended to check for any sign of wear or tear before attempting to replace the belt or the spool.

Fixing Springs and Clips

Springs and clips are important components of antique radios; they ensure that certain parts stay securely in place, while also providing a degree of flexibility. It is important to inspect the frames of these radios more closely, and to replace/repair any springs and clips which may be loose, ill-fitting, or damaged. In some cases, restoring a spring or clip requires fitting it into place with a soldering iron, or via impact energy. Installing tension clips is a delicate procedure, as the spring must not be distorted, nor should the clip be pressed too hard onto the spring. It is therefore important to adhere to the instructions provided along the repair manual for each device. Given the complexity of most antique radios, and their range of components, it is essential to understand the basics of each component before attempting any repair or replacement. Knowing which parts to repair and how to repair them can save time and effort, and help to keep restored radios functioning for many years to come. With practice and patience, anyone can become skilled at restoring antique radios, preserving a piece of history that might otherwise have been lost.

Chapter 24: Adding Accessories

Accessorizing an antique radio is a great way to give it a new look, provide additional functionality, and collect memorabilia of the era. It can improve the performance of the radio, provide customization options, and open up a world of possibilities in the area of music and entertainment. In this chapter, we will discuss the various ways you can update your antique radio with accessories such as markers, meters, and other devices.

Adding Markers and Meters

One of the most common accessories for an antique radio is the tuning meter – these were the first devices to be able to accurately measure the level of signal in the radio, helping you to easily and quickly find the correct frequency you want to listen to. Tuning meters were initially used for international shortwave broadcasts, but today they are widely used to tune in your favorite local FM radio stations. They come in both analog and digital versions, and you can use either for tuning an antique radio. Alternatively, tuner markers are available to add extra style and functionality to the radio tuning control. They come in a variety of formats, including classic illuminated and non-illuminated bezels, illuminated and non-illuminated pointer markers, and even ornamental symbols or symbols of your choosing. Not only do they add a vintage look to your radio, but they also make it easier and quicker to find the right frequency.

Assuring Voltage Steps

When you are adding accessories to an antique radio, you must make sure that the voltage supply is not too low or too high. Otherwise, the parts may be damaged or the radio may not operate correctly. To test the voltage, use a multimeter to read the voltage across the connector. Firstly, unplug the antenna and make sure the radio is off before attaching the multimeter's red clip to the positive terminal and its black to the negative. If the voltage is less than 7 volts, replace the filter capacitors and check the radio again. If the voltage is still low after replacing the capacitors, replace the tubes. If the voltage is greater than 10 volts, check the voltage regulator, and make sure there is no short circuit in the wiring.

Connecting Phonographs

Phonographs, or record players, used to be common accessories for radios and still provide an excellent way to listen to gramophone recordings. In order to connect a phono turntable to an antique radio, you need to have a phono output with enough gain for the turntable. To do this, you can use a small add-on preamp with a phono input and line-level output. However, there is a simpler way – use a "phono control", which is nothing more than a potentiometer set up to lower the signal level coming from the turntable. This will provide enough gain to drive the amplifier stage of the radio as normal but with a significantly lower signal level. When setting up the phono control, ensure the output of the turntable is appropriate for the input threshold of the radio. You should also make sure that the turntable is well-grounded and that the + and – speaker terminals are connected correctly. Overall, adding accessories to an antique radio is a great way to improve its sound quality and style. There are a range of options available – from tuners and markers to voltage regulators and phonographs – each of which provides an opportunity to further customize your radio and make it truly your own.

Chapter 25: Avoiding Disaster

Restoring an antique radio can be a perilous task. Radio repair requires a delicate touch and an intimate knowledge of the radio's inner workings. If done improperly, it can result in a destroyed vintage radio which is worth far more than its parts. For a successful antique radio restoration, several steps should be taken to avoid disaster. This chapter will outline the necessary safety procedures for constructing and maintaining a functioning antique radio.

Applying Adequate Mounting

In order to minimize the risk of damaging components, it is essential that the radio is securely mounted and is able to take the weight of the parts. If a loose connection is present, it can cause the radio to suddenly power off, leading to component damage and potential destruction of the vintage radio. To ensure that radio restoration is conducted safely, ensure that all mounts are firmly attached to the radio. If the mounting screws are loose, they should be replaced with new ones. Additionally, always use washers between the screw and the mount to help provide extra stability. Also be sure that the mount is securely tightened to the board and that no components are loose and able to short circuit or damage other components, such as wiring and tubes.

Avoiding Risky Alternatives

It is crucial to think before jumping into risky solutions. While it may be tempting to replace all of the components of the antique radio without understanding the underlying issue, this can lead to more harm than good. Some of the components in an antique radio are extremely delicate and may not be easy to find or replace. If these components are damaged due to an attempted repair, it can cause a cascade of issues and reduce the overall lifetime of the radio. Therefore, it is best to understand the issue before performing any repairs. Ask questions and identify the source of the problem before jumping into any risky solutions.

Controlling Heat

Heat can be an issue when working with vintage radios. Excessive heat can lead to component failure, so it is important to take the necessary steps to minimize heat build-up. Take frequent breaks while working on the radio and make sure to wear protective gloves to avoid burning your hands. If possible, keep a damp cloth near the radio so that it can be quickly wiped to reduce heat. When soldering, use a soldering iron with a temperature control setting and a small tip. This will reduce the risk of any heat-related damage.

Additionally, use a damp cloth to minimize the amount of smoke that the soldering iron produces. When replacing components, use a non-flammable heat sink to reduce the risk of a fire. In conclusion, there are several steps that must be taken to avoid disaster during the restoration of an antique radio. Make sure to mount the radio securely and take safety precautions when operating the radio. Take the time to understand the underlying issue before attempting to fix it and take steps to control heat build-up when working with the radio. A successful vintage radio restoration requires the utmost care and precision in order to preserve its original condition.

Chapter 26: Dial Scales

Antique radios feature a variety of dial scales for tuning and monitoring the frequency of the radio's output. These components are delicate, often defunct, and highly integral to the restoration process. In fact, a dial scale in operable condition is practically essential to any full or partial restoration of a vintage radio. In this chapter we will discuss the different structures associated with dial scales and tips for restoring them to their former glory.

Antiquated Dial Scales

In order to understand the problems associated with restoring vintage dial scales, it is important to first understand the basics of their design and purpose. Typically, a dial scale consists of two main parts, the indicator and the frequency dial. The indicator is a mechanical part that magnetically interacts with reed switches to inform the frequency the radio is receiving. The frequency dial is a carefully calibrated collection of numbers and markers that the indicator passes over to inform the user of the radio's reception. These components are often fragile due to their age, and in many instances the indicator is no longer functional or missing. Even if the physical components of the dial scale remain intact, the frequency numbers and markers can easily become corroded, marred or otherwise damaged over time.

Restoration Tips and Solutions

In many cases, a dial scale can be successfully restored with patience and a steady hand. Cleaning the application is the first step to successful restoration, as it removes any dirt, grime or corroded surfaces that can cause further damage down the line. Soapy water is an ideal cleaning solution to use on antique radio components but only if it is completely dry before any further work is done. Should the indicator prove to be non-functional, a suitable replacement can often be sourced from various vendors. It is vital to ensure the specifications of any part replaced match the original as closely as possible. This not only helps to ensure unit performance, but also guarantees that the visual aspect of the dial scale remains harmonious with the form factor of the vintage radio. It is also important to ensure that any new frequency dial is properly calibrated and sized before it is affixed to the radio. A dial with the incorrect measurements can cause difficulty for the user and may even lead to further damage to the delicate components of the vintage radio.

Another aspect of vintage dial scale restoration is the replacement of worn or corroded numbers or markers. Many experienced hobbyists successfully recreate these details on the frequency dial themselves, painstakingly hand painting the numbers and markers in order to recreate the markings accurately. Finally, when working with an antique radio, it is important to remember to take it slow. Always make sure to handle any delicate components with care, and never rush a restoration process. Taking the necessary time and care to lovingly restore a vintage radio is the best way to guarantee a successful result.

Chapter 27: Replacing Resistors

When it comes to antique radio restoration, replacing resistors is no small feat. It requires precise precision to ensure that the radio is functioning correctly, safely, and reliably. In this chapter we will discuss the process of selecting appropriate resistors, measuring resistors, and other considerations that one should take into account when replacing them.

Selecting Appropriate Resistors

When it comes to selecting resistors for a project, the most important thing to consider is the resistance of the resistor. This is especially important when it comes to radios, since the resistance must closely match the original design in order for the set to work correctly. In addition, one should also consider the power dissipation of the resistor and the voltage rating to make sure the resistor isn't being pushed beyond its limits. When selecting the resistance of the resistor, it is important to be as precise as possible. For instance, if the original resistor was rated at 22.5 ohms, a resistor with a resistance of 22 ohms will also work, but it is not recommended. It is best to be as close as possible to the original specification. In terms of power dissipation, it is important to choose a resistor that can dissipate the same amount of power or higher than the original design. If the resistor is being used in a high power application, it is wise to choose a higher power resistor. Finally, when it comes to voltage rating, it is important to choose a resistor with a voltage rating higher than the operating voltage of the circuit. This not only helps maintain the integrity of the resistor but also helps to minimize potential safety risks.

Measuring Resistors

When it comes to measuring resistors, it is necessary to ensure that the resistance of the resistor is as close to the intended value as possible. There are a few different tests that can be performed in order to measure a resistor's resistance: The first is the ohmmeter test. This requires an ohmmeter and an external resistor in order to measure accurately. The ohmmeter can be used to measure the resistance by connecting one lead to one end of the resistor and the other lead to the other end. This will give an accurate reading of the resistance. The second test is the diode test. This involves connecting a diode across the two ends of the resistor. The current will then flow in one direction and this will give an indication of the approximate resistance of the resistor. The third test is the bridge test.

This involves connecting four resistors in a bridge configuration in order to measure the resistance. This test is more accurate than the ohmmeter and diode tests and is recommended when accuracy is key. Finally, the fourth test is the Oscilloscope test. This involves connecting an oscilloscope across the resistor and measuring the voltage across the resistor. This test is more accurate than the other tests and is usually used when extremely precise measurements are required. When using any of these tests, it is important to ensure that the readings are correct. It is also worth noting that there may be slight variations in the readings due to temperature, humidity, and other factors. Therefore, it is important to take into account these factors when making measurements. Replacing resistors can be a time consuming process, but the time and effort can be well worth it to ensure that the circuit is functioning correctly, safely, and reliably.

When selecting and measuring resistors, it is important to be precise, think carefully about design considerations, and be aware of potential safety risks. By taking these factors into account, one can be sure that the circuit will be in good working order and will be safe to use.

Chapter 28: Design Considerations

When it comes to the restoration of vintage radios, proper design considerations are key to success. Knowing the principles behind vintage radio design is one of the most important aspects that must be taken into account, in order to ensure that a vintage radio is properly restored. Before diving in, however, it is important to understand the basic components of vintage radios, as well as the different types of tube topologies used in vintage radio design.

Tube Topologies

Vintage radios contain a variety of tubes, including triodes, pentodes, and even tetrodes. These tubes each have their own unique characteristics and must be taken into consideration when planning a vintage radio restoration. The most common tube topology used in vintage radio design is the triode topology. This topology utilizes three main components: the grid, the plate, and the cathode. These three elements work together to control the flow of electrons within the tube and thus control the radio signal's amplitude. A pentode topology, on the other hand, is a more complicated topology that utilizes five main components. These components are the grid, the plate, the suppressor grid, the screen grid, and the cathode. This topology is typically used in more complex vintage radios and allows for better amplification and signal control.

Shunts

Another important factor to consider when restoring vintage radios is the use of shunts. Shunts are used to provide a resistance in the signal path, thereby allowing the signal to pass through more efficiently. Shunts are typically used in conjunction with other components, such as resistors and capacitors, to ensure that a circuit is properly balanced.

Power Supply

Finally, the power supply of a vintage radio must be taken into consideration when restoring. Many vintage radios utilize an alternating current (AC) power supply, which can be dangerous to work with. An AC power supply requires components such as a transformer, rectifiers, and capacitors in order to provide the necessary power to the tube. It is important to be aware of the proper voltage and current ratings of these components when restoring a vintage radio. When restoring vintage radios, it is important to consider all of these design considerations. Taking the time to understand the principles behind vintage radio design will ensure that the project is a success. By doing so, not only will the vintage radio be restored to its former glory, but its longevity will also be extended. It may take some extra time and effort to properly restore a vintage radio, but the results will be worth it. - Just write 1000 words for Chapter 31 only.

Chapter 29: Advanced Troubleshooting

When it comes to restoring antique radios, advanced troubleshooting techniques are essential for finding hidden problems and restoring graceful vintage sound. Armed with the right tools and knowledge, anyone can get started on this rewarding journey.

Paralleling Components

Before tackling advanced troubleshooting techniques, it's important to understand the concept of parallel components. When two or more electrical components are connected in parallel, current can divide equally among the All the components. This means that all the components will have the same voltage potential. This is an important concept because it can affect circuit issues when doing advanced troubleshooting. Advanced troubleshooters will use this technique to compare and analyze differences in conductive properties between components, helping to identify faults and problems that are not immediately visible. If a component is found to not be conducting properly, replacing it with a new one may fix the problem. In some cases, components can be moved or rewired in parallel to restore the radio's original state and fix the underlying issue.

Troubleshooting Techniques

When advanced troubleshooting, the key is to look at things from multiple angles. The traditional technique involves using a VOMs (Volt-Ohm-Milliammeter) meter to measure resistance and detect any changes in conductor properties. In addition, a DMM (Digital Multimeter) can be used to measure voltage, frequency, and current for more detailed analysis. Sometimes, a simple visual inspection can reveal underlying problems. For example, you might find corrosion on a wire or a loose connection. These kinds of problems may not appear on meters or other diagnostic tools, but they still can cause serious issues. By keeping a keen eye out for these issues and making quick fixes, you can avoid more serious problems down the road.

Hotspots

When advanced troubleshooting, it's important to pay attention to hotspots – places where components become overly hot. While some heat is normal, excessive hot spots suggest there is something wrong with the circuit. It is important to identify the cause of the heat and repair it before further damage occurs. The most common cause of hotspots are malfunctioning components. These components can create a feedback loop, leading to damaging current and/or voltage rises. It could be as simple as a worn-out resistor or a faulty capacitor, so it is important to look closely at all components in order to identify the source of the problem.

Hidden Faults

Hidden faults can be one of the most difficult problems to identify when performing advanced troubleshooting. A symptom of a hidden fault can be poor performance, but there may also be no visible change in the functioning of the radio at all. Hidden faults are often caused by corrosion, oxidation, or bad wiring. They can also occur when minor problems build up over time, resulting in a breakdown. The best way to identify a hidden fault is to thoroughly inspect all components and wiring. This includes looking at exposed areas (such as knobs, dials, and buttons), testing for any hidden corrosion, and testing ohmic resistance. In some cases, it may be necessary to replace the part or components if there is no other way to restore proper functioning. Advanced troubleshooting can take some practice, but with the right tools and a little patience, anyone can undertake this rewarding journey. These techniques can be used to identify and rectify a wide variety of problems, helping to restore vintage sound and make an otherwise forgotten radio sound as good as new.

Chapter 30: Troubleshooting Tube Radios

Troubleshooting a tube radio can be a difficult process, especially for inexperienced restorers. While the same basic troubleshooting principles can be applied to both modern transistors and vacuum tubes, tube radio design presents its own set of unique challenges. To effectively troubleshoot a tube radio, an understanding of vacuum tube characteristics and the basic circuits of a tube radio are essential. This chapter will discuss how to approach troubleshooting a tube radio, with an emphasis on valve sequence, socket tests, and achieving optimum conditions.

Valving Sequence

A crucial first step in troubleshooting a tube radio is assessing the sequence of valves being used. Valves are what make a tube radio work. Depending on the model of radio, it will contain either a complex set or a basic set of valves. Depending on the complexity of the set, the valve sequence needs to be checked. To do this, it's important to first identify the type of valves being used and then trace the connections between their sockets. Any connections that are out of sequence can be adjusted to bring the radio back to working order. Another common cause of failure in a tube radio is due to the age of the valves. It's not uncommon for a vintage radio to have a small number of valves that have gone bad due to a combination of age and use. This can generally be addressed by replacing the faulty valves with ones that are of a similar model.

Socket Tests

In addition to checking the valve sequence, it's important to perform socket tests on the radio to ensure that all of the connections between the valves and the other components are secure. This is especially vital if the radio contains complex or sensitive circuits. To do this, it's important to use a multimeter to check the resistances across each of the sockets. Any resistances that are too low or high can be addressed by replacing the associated connection.

Optimum Conditions

Once the valve sequence and socket tests have been completed, it's time to begin further troubleshooting on the radio. The ideal conditions for a tube radio are for all of the functions to operate continuously without any pauses or glitches. If any of the functions are hindered, then the radio needs to be adjusted to achieve the optimal performance. This might include changing the electrical components, such as resistors or capacitors, or replacement of valves or tubes. If the radio still appears to be in functional disarray, then it may be necessary to take a closer look at the circuitry used in the radio. In most cases, the radio circuits contain simple resistor-capacitor networks that amplify the signal.

If the circuit is overly complex to the point that it can't be easily understood, then it's likely time to consult a professional. The best approach to troubleshooting a tube radio is to proceed methodically and systematically. By checking the valve sequence, socket tests, and ensuring optimum conditions, it should be possible to identify and resolve the majority of issues that may be encountered. Taking the time to methodically work through the process can save considerable time and effort in the long run.

Chapter 31: Troubleshooting Valve Amplifiers

Valve amplifiers are powerful pieces of technology that provide rich, amplified audio for a variety of purposes. Because of this, troubleshooting them can be tricky, requiring the knowledge and experience to identify and solve issues. In this chapter, we'll take a look at some of the common faults and solutions for valve amplifiers, and discuss reactances, adjusting voltages, resonance, and feedback.

Reactances

Reactance is the opposition a component has to alternating current caused by inductance or capacitance. In valve amplifiers, reactance is often caused by plates, tubes, and coils. This can interfere with the signal, affecting the amplifier's performance. To troubleshoot this, use an ohmmeter to test the reactance between interconnected parts, and check for variations when moving the valve within its mount. If the indicative readings remain constant, it may be caused by aging and replaced components.

Adjusting Voltages

Valve amplifiers require the correct voltage in order to perform at their best. With varying tube sensitivities, adjusting these voltages can be a tricky process, as too low and too high an electrical current can both cause issues. To prevent issues or rectify them, use a regulated, high quality power transformer and ensure the necessary voltages for each tube type are accurate.

Resonance And Feedback

The resonance of a valve amplifier represents the frequency at which it amplifies sound. This can be affected by an amplifier's feedback loop, which is a system of interconnected parts that continually monitor the electrical performance and modify it accordingly. When troubleshooting a valve amplifier, it's important to check the feedback loop and adjust accordingly to ensure the best signal impact. By identifying reactances, adjusting voltages and understanding resonance and feedback, it's possible to troubleshoot and correctly calibrate a valve amplifier. However, due to their complexity and support of a wide range of tube types and sensitivities, the effect of faulty components can vary. As such, it's important to conduct thorough testing and troubleshooting of the entire system, before making any adjustments. Finally, it's also worth noting that valve amplifier restoration and repair is an extremely delicate and intricate process, so having adequate knowledge and experience is key to avoiding costly mistakes or errors.

Chapter 32: Distortion Identification

Types of Distortion

Distortion is one of the biggest enemies of antique radio restoration. Identifying and resolving distortion in antique radios is not always easy, as the cause can be something mundane such as a faulty part, or it could be due to something more complicated such as current leakage. The types of distortion can range from mild harmonic distortion to severe clipping. Harmonic distortion is caused by the addition of harmonics, which are extra frequencies that sound harsh and unpleasant. This type of distortion is usually lower in level than the fundamental signal, and can be brought under control quite easily with a few simple changes. Intermodulation distortion is caused when two or more signals interact and cause a third signal to be generated. It can be heard as a distorted sound coming from a loudspeaker or radio speaker. If this type of distortion is present in an antique radio, then it is best to replace the transistors or valves, or to re-tune the radio altogether.

Transient distortion is caused by signals that are suddenly changed or disrupted, causing a noticeable audible change. This can be caused by failing components or poorly adjusted components, and can often be heard as a high-pitched whine or buzzing. Transient distortion can be eliminated by changing or replacing the faulty part, or by adjusting the levels correctly. Clipping is also a common type of distortion and occurs when the signal's amplitude is beyond the range that can be handled by the amplifier. This often results in a harsh, clipped sound, which is hard to eliminate without taking the amplifier apart and making adjustments.

Resolving Issues with Output Transformers

The output transformer is a very important component in an antique radio and can cause distortion if it is not working correctly. If the output transformer is faulty, then it may be necessary to look for any shorted turns or breaks in the wiring. If a short circuit is detected, then it is best to replace the transformer with a new one. It is also important to test the output transformer with an oscilloscope to ensure that it is producing a clean signal. If there are distortions in the signal, then the output transformer should be replaced. The amp must also be properly wired to make sure that the power is being delivered to the correct part of the circuit.

Also, make sure that the transformer connections are clean and secure. Cleaning the connections can help to reduce any hum or interference being produced by the output transformer. It may also be necessary to check the insulation around the connections, as this can break down over time, causing distortion. Finally, it is important to test the radio or amplifier at different volumes to see how it responds to different inputs. Listening tests are quite useful for identifying any issues with the output transformer. If the amplifier is distorting at a low level, then it could be a sign that the output transformer is faulty.

Chapter 33: Valving Modification

The restoration of old radios can be a thrilling process that brings back to life a forgotten part of history. It is also a complicated process that requires knowledge of electrical components and repair techniques to ensure that the radio works correctly as intended. Valving modification is one such repair process that is necessary when restoring vintage radios. This chapter focuses on the different techniques and processes for modifying the valves in antique radios.

Re-Biasing Circuits

When restoring a vintage radio, the valve circuit must be re-biased to ensure that the current is not too great. Re-biasing is also necessary to adjust the tube operating conditions for optimum performance. To re-bias the circuit, the plate and grid voltages are adjusted and the cathode resistor is changed to the appropriate value. This process requires the use of a special tool known as a bias meter. The technician must have expertise with electrical components in order to read and interpret the bias meter readings.

Troubleshooting Poor Valving

Valve tubes can often become noisy or weak over time and need to be replaced or adjusted. A technician must pay attention to the output signal of the radio as it can change depending on the valves that are installed. Poor and noisy valving can also be caused by an issue with AC hum, RF RF and hum caused by bad insulation or faulty circuits, or loose connectors and wires. In order to pinpoint the source of the issue, the technician must analyze the entire circuit and check the tubes for any signs of damage or deterioration.

Employing Spray Cleaners

In addition to re-biasing the circuits and troubleshooting poor valves, the technician must also clean the valves and circuits. When dealing with dusty and dirty valves, a technician should use special spray cleaners to gently clean away the dirt, oil and other debris. It is important to never use cleaning solvents on valves as these can be harmful. The technician should also carefully check for any signs of corrosion and discoloration that may be present due to improper storage techniques. In addition to the techniques discussed above, technicians may also re-tube valves, replace bad parts, perform transformer tests and repairs, and re-tune the radio. The process of restoring an old radio can be lengthy and require patience, however the thrill of bringing the radio back to life is unmatched. Valving Modification is an essential part of the process and must be undertaken carefully and diligently in order to ensure the integrity of the radio and its vintage sound.

Chapter 34: Solving Common Problems

Restoring antique radios can be a challenge due to the age and wear of the radio, but with the right techniques and knowledge it can be achievable. In this chapter we explore common issues that arise when restoring antique radios and discuss techniques for troubleshooting and solving them.

SWR Issues

When trying to diagnose problems with an antique radio, one of the first things to check is the Standing Wave Ratio, or SWR. This measures the amount of energy returned to the transmitter or receiver, and a low ratio typically means the antenna is working properly. Interference and interference issues can also cause an SWR measurement to rise, indicating that the antenna may be tuned incorrectly or giving off an unintended signal. To troubleshoot an SWR issue, first disconnect the antenna from the receiver and see if there is any change in the reading. If the measurement stays the same without the antenna connected, then the issue may be with the receiver. In this case the tuner may need to be adjusted, or the receiver may need to be recalibrated. If the SWR goes down when the antenna is disconnected then the issue may be with the antenna. In this case, checking for loose connections, adding shielding to the antenna, or replacing components may be necessary.

Bad Connections

Bad connections in a radio can cause performance issues, including interference and distortion. In some cases the issue may even prevent the radio from working altogether. Poor connections can occur in the antenna, or within any of the various components of a radio. To fix a bad connection, start by checking the antenna connection. Make sure the antenna is securely connected to the receiver and no wires are loose or frayed. If the connection is good, then wind the antenna manually and see if that helps. If the antenna is not the problem then it may be a faulty wiring connection in one of the components. Start by probing the pins of each component with an ohmmeter in order to detect any breaks in the circuit. Then use a soldering iron to make the necessary repairs. If there is any corrosion on the components then clean off the corrosion before soldering.

Blown Fuses

Faulty electrical connections often result in blown fuses. To fix a blown fuse in an antique radio, first check the fuse for damage. Fuses can be damaged by a high current or voltage, or even by age. If the fuse is damaged then it needs to be replaced. If the fuse looks intact then it may not need to be replaced. Instead try a resistance test to check for breaks, then solder the connections together. Blown fuses may also be caused by old components or a high resistance. If any of the components in the circuit are faulty replace them. If the resistance is too high, then investigate why and correct the issue. When restoring an antique radio, it is important to identify and solve the common problems that arise. By troubleshooting the SWR issues, bad connections, and blown fuses, an antique radio can be restored to its original condition and enjoyed for many more years to come.

Chapter 35: Repairing Capacitors

Antique radios require considerable restoration and maintenance in order to stay in good condition and working properly. One important part of that process is repair and replacement of capacitors. This chapter will explain the basics of capacitor maintenance, inspection, and replacement.

Checking for Faulty or Leaky Capacitors

Before repairing or replacing capacitors, it's important to determine why they need to be repaired or replaced, and to check for short or faulty capacitors. To check for shorted or faulty capacitors, use an ohm-meter. If the reading on the ohm-meter is close to zero, the capacitor is shorted and needs to be replaced. If the ohm-meter reading is high, the capacitor is likely open or leaking and needs to be replaced. It's also important to inspect capacitors for discoloration or burning, as this indicates the capacitor is overheated and should be replaced. Overheating can be caused by faulty connections or electrolyte leakage. Capacitors can be inspected further by measuring the voltage. If the reading is below the maximum rated value, the capacitor is faulty and needs to be replaced.

Replacing Capacitors

When it comes to replacing capacitors, it's important to use a compatible capacitor. It is just as important to use a capacitor with the same value of capacity (or higher), but lower in the maximum working voltage. Depending on the application, some capacitors are polarized and must be replaced with a part with the same polarity. Before purchasing capacitors, it is important to evaluate the parts in the context of their price, performance, and long-term reliability. As vintage radio restoration projects are often long-term, one should understand the cost/benefit implications of selecting different capacitor types. It is also important to take note of capacitor ratings and features.

A capacitor's features will determine the type of applications for which it is best suited. For example, some capacitors are designed for better high-frequency stability and have higher maximum voltage ratings than others. For antique radios, the most important features are temperature stability and dielectric strength. It is important to consider the application environment (high temperature, humid locations, etc.) before selecting capacitors. When installing new capacitors, it is important to use the proper tools and techniques. Some techniques, such as matching balun installation, require particular care and attention. Baluns must be properly secured, as improper installation can lead to incorrect voltage readings or component failure.

Proper attention must also be given to the temperature ratings of all components, as temperature can have an effect on component operation and longevity. Additionally, all wiring must be properly routed and insulated to avoid unnecessary degradation or failure. Once installed, capacitors require care and maintenance. Some capacitors should be stored in a dry environment, away from heat and moisture, and given periodic testing to ensure proper operation. Other capacitors should be cleaned and lubricated periodically, or replaced when worn or faulty. Above all, antique radio restoration projects require attention to detail and a respect for the delicate equipment. Not all capacitors are alike, and the appropriate capacitor type, value, and features must be carefully evaluated to avoid component failure or damage. With the proper tools, training, and time, anyone can restore their vintage radio and ensure its proper operation for years to come.

Printed in Great Britain
by Amazon